Silent Night, Silent Guns: The 1914 Christmas Truce

British soldiers carrying mistletoe, Christmas 1914.
The Illustrated War News, 30 December 1914.

Silent Night, Silent Guns: The 1914 Christmas Truce

by

TIMOTHY J. DEMY

Stone Tower Press

Frontispiece: Library of Congress

ISBN: 979-8-9868172-0-0

Originally printed privately in December 2014. Revised edition, 2022

Designed by Scott J. Vile at the Ascensius Press

Contents

Preface

IT was called the Great War but it might just as easily have been named the Great Tragedy. Much that occurred in the war was unexpected, including the use of new weapons and warfare on a scale never before seen in history. The static warfare experienced by the soldiers of the Western Front meant long periods of close proximity to the enemies in miserable conditions shared by all. It was in the midst of these common depredations that the Christmas truce arose during the war's first Christmas season as kindred spirits created an informal truce.

British spellings and punctuation have been kept as have varied systems of naming regimental units. In their letters, soldiers speak for themselves without correction of spelling, punctuation, or fact.

Background and Beginnings

"PEACE ON EARTH, GOOD WILL TO MEN"—so declared the angels to astonished shepherds, according to St. Luke's Gospel. But this year, 1914, there was no peace. There was only war. Across the wet and frozen fields of Flanders and France, hundreds of thousands of soldiers faced one another in mortal combat. "Good will" was exchanged for "good shot." The best gift soldiers might wish for this night of Christmas Eve was to live to see the dawn.

On the first Christmas centuries earlier, shepherds in the fields watching their sheep had been surprised by angels and were afraid. This night, soldiers in their trenches were watching their enemies, and they, too, were afraid. All eyes were not on heavenly hosts. They were on earthly armies. It was not a brilliant star that filled and illuminated the nighttime sky, but starburst flares lighting battlefields.

The war was supposed to be over. When declarations of war were proclaimed in capitals across Europe during the lazy and waning days of summer in August 1914, thousands of people joyously marched in the streets of London, Paris, and Berlin. Aristocrats, business magnates, and national leaders watched and waved from balconies above in their finest attire—khaki had not yet replaced couture. There was an atmosphere of anticipation and excitement. Workers believed the annual fortnight holiday that shuttered shops and factories would be extended, this year by a few weeks or perhaps months because of the war. It might not be a holiday, but it would be an adventure.

"Over by Christmas" had been the consensus. It was pure folly. What was supposed to be a war of mobility quickly turned into a static war of attrition. As days turned to weeks and weeks to months, so too did the lines of armies stretch across the map of Europe like an outstretched arm grasping for safety. The "race to the sea" was the pundits' phrase used to describe the strategy wherein allied British and French forces tried to outflank, to the west, German forces marching toward Paris, creating "the Western Front." It spanned nearly five hundred miles, from Switzerland to the English Channel and North Sea.

They did not know it in August 1914, or even by December 1914, but over the course of the war from 1914-1918, the front would shift by only a few miles at most as the armies bloodied one another like two boxers locked in a weary and deadly fight. Trench lines established in 1914 moved no more than eleven miles.[1] It was this strategic stalemate that would later prompt First Lord of the Admiralty Winston Churchill to ask: "Are there not other alternatives than sending our armies to chew barbed wire in Flanders?"[2] This Christmas, there were not.

Christmas truce (German: *Weihnachtsfrieden;* French: *Trêve de Noël*) is the name given to a series of unofficial and unconnected ceasefires that occurred along the Western Front during the Christmas season of 1914. It is estimated that as many as 100,000 troops participated. In many places along the front, the Christmas truce was foreshadowed on Christmas Eve by German and British soldiers singing carols of both sides and by the Germans placing Christmas trees lit by paper lanterns and candles on the parapets of their trenches. According to one British soldier viewing them across No Man's Land, the lights looked "like lights of a theatre."[3]

The truce occurred mainly in the British sector on the south edge of the Ypres Salient between St Éloi and La Bassée. There are estimates that as much as two-thirds of the British sector experienced the truce in one form or another, and the acrid smell of cordite was replaced by the wafting aroma of tobacco as enemies shared cigarettes and cigars.[4] Most of the episodes occurred on December 24th, 25th, and 26th, but there were instances of the truce lasting until New Year's Day 1915.

Though it became known as the "Christmas truce," not every soldier on the Western Front experienced it. Most French and Belgian troops were in no mood for such a thing (although some did participate). Neutral Belgium had been invaded and overrun by German soldiers who then struck France and attempted to reach Paris in hopes of a quick knockout victory. But the British had come to the aid of Belgium and France. In the late summer and early fall of 1914 the British Expeditionary Force (BEF) had fought a while withdrawing from Mons, retreating to the Marne in order to keep in contact with

French forces who were hoping to protect Paris from capture by the Germans. Those engagements of the Battle of the Frontiers and race westward toward the North Sea had now come to an end and battle lines were hardening. It was these lines of the Western Front that soldier novelist Henry Williamson wrote of, in *The Phoenix Generation,* as "that great livid wound that lay across Europe suppurating during more than fifteen hundred nights and days."

By December 1914, approximately 40,000 British soldiers had lost their lives, and French and Belgian casualties neared 400,000. In mid-December, the British initiated a series of costly attacks on German positions at Ploegstreet Wood—"Plugstreet" to the Tommies—hoping to provoke an aggressive response. Losses were significant, including many from misdirected artillery fire using shells imported from pre-war Germany. Leading up to Christmas Day, large numbers of the dead remained unburied, many hanging on barbed wire designed to protect the trenches. The soldiers' song was becoming much too familiar visually as well as musically:

> If you want to find the old battalion,
> I know where they are. . . .
> They're hanging on the old barbed wire.[5]

It seemed as if the only celebration this Christmas was a celebration of death. On December 20th, French forces started a major counterattack in the Champagne region. Attack and counterattack—it was a preview of coming attractions in this theater of war.

No one knows exactly where it started, but at points all along the Western Front, like-minded soldiers emerged from the relative safety of the trenches and dugouts and entered the killing zone of No Man's Land, the areas separating enemy trenches and barren of all but shell craters and barbed wire. The spontaneity was as unexpected as it was remarkable. The majority of the reported instances and eyewitness accounts come from one sector of the front, although it was not limited there. Most eyewitness accounts credited the Germans with initiating meetings in No Man's Land to negotiate for individual ceasefires. For example, one British soldier wrote that on "Xmas Day we heard the words 'Happy Christmas!' being called out, wherefore we wrote up on a board 'Gluckliches Werhnnachten!' and stuck it up. There was no firing, so by degrees each side began gradually showing more of themselves, and then two of their men came halfway over and called for an officer."[6] While there were many instances of fraternization, for some troops there was only a ceasefire.

Some things about the truce are well known and others, not. As one soldier's letter stated: "There is heaps more I should like to tell, but I know it would never get passed [along by the censors] so it will have to wait."[7] Whether that soldier survived the war is unknown. Just as there was no single war experience shared by all of the millions of soldiers in uniform, neither was there a single truce experienced by those who participated in the December 1914 cessation of hostilities. Soldiers had different experiences of the truce and some none at all. Those soldiers who did experience the truce were professional soldiers of the British Expeditionary Force. These were not the soldiers of the large conscript army that was to come, but rather career soldiers and reservists and some Territorials, and this too may have fostered a spirit of tolerance at Christmas. Diaries, letters, unit histories, newspaper accounts, and official documents presented a kaleidoscope of information that in particulars and totality looked different for every person viewing the event.

British newspapers (and even American ones) were quick to publish accounts of the truce and cite from letters written by soldiers to friends and family at home. News from the front was strictly controlled by the government and so, in addition to official government reports and press releases, newspapers turned to their readers for human interest stories, soliciting letters received by family and friends by soldiers at the front. Fortunately, these published accounts survived even though many of the letters are no longer extant.

Often written in pencil on paper exposed to the mud and harsh conditions of trench life, the letters showed that the soldiers understood that they were participants in a unique event. As Lance Corporal Cooper of the 2nd Northamptons wrote to his wife in a letter published in *The Bedfordshire Times and Independent*, "Now who would believe it if they did not see it with their own eyes? It is hard enough for us to believe."[8]

"English, you no shoot, we no shoot." With these words, one group of German soldiers initiated their truce on Christmas Eve—in the spirit of the season, but also probably for a brief but safe respite from the drudgery of daily life in the trenches. German trenches were considered better than those of the British, but they were still ditches and dugouts.

Life in the trenches was miserable. Often, soldiers constructed the trenches quickly and with haphazard placement when they were unable to advance. Sometimes they were little more than connected shell craters and foxholes that, in time, became larger and an interconnected maze for the men who lived a mole-like existence in them. The trenches were poorly constructed and subject to frequent flooding in the muddy and flat areas of Flanders and France. During the war, the British army alone issued more than ten-and-a-half million spades, prompting one soldier to proclaim, "I enlisted to save France, not to shovel it into sacks."[9]

Much of the marshy land of the Ypres Salient was below sea level and often flooded; the water table began about eighteen inches below the surface. It was in conditions such as this that C. S. Lewis, an infantry officer in 1917-1918, remembered:

> Through the winter, weariness and water were our chief enemies. I have gone to sleep marching and

> woken again marching still. One walked in the trenches in thigh gum boots with water above the knee; one remembers the icy stream welling up inside the boot when you punctured it on concealed barbed wire. [There was] familiarity with both the very old and the very recent dead....[10]

These words echoed the sentiment of A. D. Chater who wrote from the trenches in a January 1915 letter that it "must be a sort of second Venice. When you find a piece of dry land you think there must be some sort of mistake – I was up to my waist in water two or three days ago."[11]

The weather favored neither side. In December, German soldier Friedrich Nickolaus, of the 53rd Reserve Pioneer Company, returned to his company after recovering from an earlier wound. He described the conditions in which he and his comrades found themselves:

> Things have got very much worse: Flanders is just one great morass and all military operations have been brought to a standstill by the mud. Day and night we stand up to our knees in mud and water. We have to wrap our legs up to our thighs in sandbags just to survive. The rain pours incessantly from above, while beneath us the water-table has risen to just below ground level.... On top of all this the mad gun-battle goes on across this forsaken plain, stretching out in front of us as flat as a table-top, where it is dangerous even to raise your head above ground during the day.[12]

In one published letter home, a member of the Royal Engineers wrote:

> December 24th: I found my section in the firing trench on day work, draining the trench, making traverses, and generally improving the position. Distance from the German firing line 240 yards, occupied by the 158th Regiment of Infantry. It was freezing hard all day. In some places we were up to our knees in clay, and a foot up our overcoats, it had frozen hard on, and our trousers and coats were like boards.[13]

Although many people think of snow at Christmas, for theses soldiers it was mixed with ice, sleet, water, and rain, with nothing festive about it. And not everyone favored even the possibility of a truce.

On 2 December 1914, Lieutenant General Sir Horace Smith-Dorrian, who commanded one of the two Corps that comprised the British Expeditionary Force, recorded in his diary:

> Weird stories come in from the trenches about fraternizing with the Germans. They shout to each other and offer to exchange certain articles. In one place, by arrangement, a bottle was put out between the trenches and then they held a competition as to which could break it first. There is a danger of opposing troops becoming too friendly, but it is only too likely to happen and it happened in the Peninsula. I therefore intend to issue instructions to my Corps not to frater-

> nize in any way with the enemy for fear one day they may be lulled into such a state of confidence as to be caught off their guard and rushed.[14]

The "Peninsula" to which he referred was the Peninsular War of 1807-1814, a long war in Spain between the British forces of the Duke of Wellington and Franco-Spanish forces of Napoleon, during which there were reports of temporary truces and fraternization. Similar instances occurred during the Crimean War (1853-1856), the American Civil War (1861-1865), the Second Boer War (1899-1902), and the Russo-Japanese War (1904-1905).

Perhaps it was to be expected that such a truce would occur once more. As one published report from the front stated:

> When ice-cold slush filled the bottoms of the trenches it was found impossible to prevent the men, when their officers were not watching them, from arranging informal truces with their enemies so they could sit up on the edge of the trenches and get their feet out of the freezing mixture. Sometimes by mutual consent the soldiers on both sides come out to mend their breastworks, working openly between the lines a couple of hundred yards apart and then getting under cover to resume firing on one another.[15]

The same report quoted a British officer's account of the situation:

> When I got back to our trenches after dark on Christmas Eve I found the Bosches' trenches looking like the Thames on Henley Regatta Night! They had got little Christmas trees burning all along the parapet of their trench. No truce had been proclaimed and I was all for not allowing the blighters to enjoy themselves, especially as they had killed one of our men that afternoon. But my captain (who hadn't seen our wounded going mad and slowly dying outside the German trenches on the Aisne) wouldn't let me shoot; however I soon had an excuse, as one of the Germans fired at us, so I quickly lined up my platoon and had those Christmas trees down and out.[16]

However, his response of firing on the enemy was not the usual one that evening. British troops were surprised to see German trenches starting to light up. In a war where striking a match or smoking a cigarette was apt to draw fire, lights were unexpected. J. Selby Grigg wrote that "(s)oon after dusk on the 24th the Germans put up lanterns on the top of their trenches and started singing, and their shooting practically ceased."[17] Even so, not all Germans were comfortable with the thought of a truce. Ludwig Renn, a young officer near the front, received orders for his unit to go to the rear, only to have them countermanded by his captain, who told him on the field telephone: "The French realize that Christmas is, for the Germans, a great festive day and they might turn to account precisely this night."[18]

Captain Josef Sewald of the 17th Bavarians initiated

the truce in his part of the line. "I shouted to our enemies that we didn't want to shoot and that we [should] make a Christmas truce."[19] From all reports, it was almost always the Germans who initiated the truce. At this point in the war they were winning and had every reason to be optimistic, believing the war would soon end and often telling the British, "*England kaput!*"[20]

Corporal Leon Harris of the 13th Battalion London Regiment (Kensington) quit his job at the famous London department store Selfridges and enlisted on 7 August 1914 as soon as war was declared. He wrote of lights and trees: "We were in the trenches on Christmas Eve, and about 8.30 the firing was almost at a stand still. Then the Germans started shouting across to us, 'A happy Christmas' and commenced putting up lots of Christmas trees with hundreds of candles on the parapets of their trenches."[21]

Dr. Frederick George Chandler, a lieutenant in the Royal Army Medical Corps serving as acting medical officer to the 2nd Battalion Argyll and Sutherland Highlanders in the trenches at Houplines, near Armentiéres, wrote of his Christmas Eve experience:

> Last night was Christmas Eve. It was a bright starry moonlit night and it froze hard. Opposite our trenches was perfect quiet and soon we began to hear the shouts of our men to the Germans and their replies. Then various musical instruments began, and song and ribald mirth. One of our sergeants got out of the trench and met one of the Germans halfway. He lived in Scotland and spoke English with a Scotch accent! They shook

> hands and exchanged hats, the German declaring they had no wish to be fighting the English.[22]

One unnamed soldier's letter home that was published in a local newspaper stated:

> On Christmas Eve at 4 p.m. we had orders that unless the 'enemy' advanced we were not to fire, and the same applied to Christmas Day. Whether the Germans had the same order or not I don't know but no shot was fired on either side. On Christmas Eve we shouted 'Compliments of the Season' to each other, and passed pleasant remarks. We sang the *Austrian Anthem* and they replied with *God Save the King*.[23]

Singing was an oft-reported activity of the truce. Sometimes the music was carols while in other instances it was popular or patriotic music. In some places it was not the sounds of music that was exchanged; it was food lobbed into the opposing trenches.[24]

Many soldiers thought the lights, singing, and Christmas trees in the German trenches on Christmas Eve were a sign of peace to come, if not in the larger sense, at least for the coming day or days—and they were right. One officer in the 1st Battalion Hampshire Regiment wrote to his parents, "(s)ure enough, the carols of Christmas Eve were followed by friendly exchange of greetings on Christmas morning. During the day both sides came out and fraternized inbetween the lines, buried stale corpses and reconoitred [*sic*] the ground."[25]

Perhaps Corporal Leon Harris summarized it best in his letter home: "It was a wonderful time and the weather was glorious on Christmas Eve and Christmas Day—frosty and bright with moon and stars at night."[26]

Christmas Day

It was a Christmas Day never to be forgotten by those who experienced it. Dr. Frederick George Chandler wrote to his sister: "This morning it was still freezing hard but a heavy mist was over everything. . . . In the afternoon all firing ceased about our lines and an extraordinary thing occurred. Our men and the Germans got out of the trenches and met each other and chatted in great groups. The Germans in fact brought a barrel of beer over to the Regt on out left! One could walk about anywhere with safety—it was a most delicious feeling I can tell you."[27]

Lance Corporal Cooper of the 2nd Northamptons wrote in a letter: "Just after one o'clock on Christmas morning I was on look-out duty and one of the Germans wished me Good morning and a Merry Christmas. I was never more surprised in my life when daylight came to see them all sitting on top of the trenches waving their hands and singing to us."[28]

Another Tommy had a similar experience:

> During the early part of the morning the Germans started singing and shouting, all in good English. They shouted out: "Are you the Rifle Brigade; have you a spare bottle; if so we will come half way and you come the other half." At 4 a.m. part of their Band played some Christmas carols and *God save the King*, and *Home Sweet Home*. You could guess our feelings. . . . I shook hands with some of them, and they gave us cigarettes and cigars.[29]

Up and down the line soldiers were experiencing an unexpected but welcomed respite from the war. Some sang, some sought souvenirs, some smoked. Rifleman J. Reading reported: "On Christmas Day after service in the trenches, we went halfway and we shook hands, and had a fine crack with them. Quite a number of them speak English. I got one's autograph and he got mine, and I exchanged a button with another and exchanged cigs and got cigars galore."[30]

Cigars and cigarettes were not the only things exchanged. Aiden Liddell, of the 93rd Argyle and Sutherland Highlanders, wrote to his parents: "This afternoon the Germans (who are a Saxon regiment opposite here) started proceedings by rolling two barrels of beer into our trenches."[31]

As they conversed, British troops were often surprised both by the attitudes of some of the Germans and by the misinformation they were hearing. Rifleman C. H. Brazier, Queen's Westminsters, wrote:

> On Christmas Day we all got out of the trenches and walked about with the Germans, who, when asked if they were fed up with the war said "Yes, rather". They all believed London had been captured, and that German sentries were outside Buckingham Palace. They were evidently told a lot of rot. We gave them some of our newspapers to convince them.[32]

What soldiers from both sides of the war found on Christmas Day was a shared humanity and that on both ends of the rifle men were the same. "Altogether we spent a very pleasant two hours with them, and found them a nice lot of fellows"[33] One newspaper summarized the day well: "It was a day of peace in war. It is only a pity that it was not a decisive peace."[34]

Regrettably, the informal truce was not always observed. C. G. V. Wellesley, who served with 2nd Battalion Lincolnshire Regiment, wrote "on our right and left they have been going on fighting as usual"[35] and H. J. Chappell also reported that, during the truce, "we could hear firing on both flanks and the artillery were bombarding each other over our heads."[36] In spite of the temporary armistice, therefore, the soldiers were unable to forget the war and were aware that, while they were fraternizing with the Germans, others were still fighting them and perhaps being wounded or killed on Christmas Day. W. H. Diggle wrote in a letter home that the Germans in his area had asked for a truce on Christmas Day but failed to uphold it. He wrote that the enemy shot "one of our officers dead who was doing his half of the truce." Diggle angrily declared that the Germans "are dirty dogs and you can't trust them."[37]

Boxing Day and Beyond

The truce was not a one-day event. For soldiers in the trenches its extension was a blessing. A Royal Engineer wrote home: "December 26.—This turned out to be another day of peace. . . . if only Kaiser Bill and other big chiefs could only agree the same as Tommy Atkins and the German soldiers we could soon have peace all the world over."[38] The same soldier was surprised to find a German speaking fluent English:

> A German came up with a loaf of black bread and three cigars, and asked if we would exchange for an English paper, as they had so many lies in theirs. We gave them a *Daily Mail,* and it contained news of the riots in Berlin. The chap could speak perfect English and told us he had a wife and three children in Liverpool.[39]

At least one unnamed soldier believed that a second day without fighting would lead to others:

> "This morning war has broken out again, but not in front of us. It is a rum show."[40] Overly optimistic, he continued: "I believe politicians will be wrong now, and that the war will come to an end because every one will get fed up and refuse to go on shooting!"[41]

In the days after Christmas, the weather reverted from snow and frost to rain, sleet, and storms, and the truce dwindled and gradually deteriorated just as had the weather. The harsh and oppressive realities of trench life continued and wounded soldiers were often as concerned with the possibility drowning as with receiving prompt medical attention. One soldier recalled Boxing Day as a day when there was some return to warfare:

> 8:40 am one of our Officers tells them [German soldiers] to get back in their trenches as our artillery are going to shell them at 9 am. Some of them say "we will get in your trenches we shall be safer". This will stop the football match. Shells are exchanged for a few hours but we all stand up at intervals, no fear of being shot with a bullet. Of course our artillery are a long way from us, same as theirs is from them, so they know nothing about our little holiday.[42]

All peace is temporal.

Food and Festivities

It was Napoleon Bonaparte who said "an army marches on its stomach." Soldiers of the Great War were no different than their predecessors. Soldiers fought on their stomachs and food was an important part of life and morale for every person in the trenches. It was common for soldiers to share food parcels from home, and Christmas parcels were especially desirable for the war's first Christmas. "It was a ripping parcel and we had a grand time over it. . . . we combined and invited four more pals, one of whom had a box of Tom Smith's Christmas crackers sent out, which we cracked, and it added to the fun immensely. Christmas in the trenches!"[43]

Dr. Frederick George Chandler recorded in his diary: "For dinner tonight [December 25th] we had soup, white wine, haggis, whisky and vegetables, some sort of old fowl, Christmas pudding with rum, savoury, dry biscuits and café au rhum."[44] Elsewhere, another British officer said of the activities he experienced in No Man's Land: "Several of the Saxons spoke fair English, and some hailed from London, much to our cockneys' delight, and talk became general about 'Peecadeely,' etc. One of them played a mouth-organ, and the others did sort of weird dances, or series of hops, in the turnip field where we were!"[45] They also traded food—sometimes, English jam for German beer. While many Germans (and British) would have liked the legendary coarse English orange marmalade, the British at the front had only cheap plum-and-apple to barter.

Germans speaking English was a common theme in letters and reports of the truce. Their linguistic abilities can be explained in part by the fact that, unlike their British counterparts, many of the German units were reserve forces comprised of young men who had worked in Britain until they were recalled to active service. It was not uncommon for British soldiers in proximity to the German trenches to call out "Waiter!" based on the fact that there had been many pre-war Germans working in British hotels and restaurants.[46]

The war diary of Captain Robert Hamilton of 1st Battalion of the Royal Warwickshire Regiment recorded many details of the truce as well as the months before and after it. Part of his account of Christmas Day tells of meeting a German chef. "The chef of the Trocadero was among the Saxons in front of us, and he seemed quite delighted to meet some of his former clients."[47] This was indeed remarkable. On 04 June 1914, two months before the war erupted, Hamilton had attending a regimental dining out celebration at the famous Trocadero Restaurant ("The Troc") in Piccadilly, London. On that occasion, Hamilton recorded in his diary that, as was customary, after the dinner they called out the head chef and gave him a cigar and five-year-old German wine from the world-famous *Bernkasteler Doctor* vineyard with the laudatory words "'Capital effort, Herr Chef! The Ris de Veau royal was quite splendid.'"[48]

British soldiers reported sharing plum pudding and rum with German troops. One soldier wrote home that:

"It would have made a good chapter in Dickens *Christmas Carol.*" He was probably right. Coincidence and humor were all part of the experiences of the day. A British soldier from High Holborn, London, was reported to have met his German barber between the lines and received a haircut. For others it was a time to frolic without fear of death. It was for many a festive and reflective time, for as one Tommy recorded in his diary: "It doesn't seem right to be killing each other at Xmas time."[49]

Music and Merriment

The hand-painted sign above the German trenches was clear:

> "CONCERT OVER HERE TONIGHT.
> ALL BRITISH TROOPS WELCOME."[50]

What was uncertain was how the British troops reading it across No Man's Land would respond.

Music, especially the singing of Christmas carols, was prominent in the letters home. At a time when most singing was in conjunction with the cadence of men marching and boots pounding the ground, the air was instead filled with songs of home and the holiday. Rifleman Graham Williams wrote of sentries first being surprised at seeing German Christmas trees with lights on the parapet of the German trench. The sentries "quickly awoke those on duty, asleep in the shelters, to 'come and see this thing, which had come to pass'" [Luke 2:15].[51] For Williams, what followed was equally surprising:

> Then our opponents began to sing "*Stille Nacht, Heilige Nacht.*" This was actually the first time I heard this carol, which was not then so popular in this country. They finished their carol and we thought that we ought to retaliate in some way, so we sang "The First Nowell," and when we finished that they all began clapping; and then they struck up another favorite of

> theirs, "*O Tannenbaum.*" And so it went on. First the Germans would sing one of their carols and then we would sing one of ours, until when we started up "O Come All Ye Faithful" the Germans immediately joined in singing the same hymn to the Latin words "*Adeste Fideles.*" And I thought, well, this was really a most extraordinary thing – two nations both singing the same carol in the middle of a war."[52]

Reports from other units of singing were much the same and included patriotic songs as well as carols. Rifleman Ernest Morely of the Queen's Westminster Rifles wrote:

> We had decided to give the Germans a Christmas present of three carols and three rifle rounds rapid. Accordingly as soon as night fell we started and the strains of "While Shepherds Watched" (beautifully rendered by the choir) arose upon the air. We finished that and paused preparatory to giving the second item on the programme. But lo! We heard answering strains from their lines.... At midnight we sang "God Save the King" and with the exception of the sentries turned in.[53]

In a letter written on Christmas Eve, Captain R. J. Armes, of the 1st Staffordshire Regiment, recounted the music he heard once the informal truce began:

> I got on top of the trench and talked German and asked them to sing a German *Volkslied* [folk song], which they did, then our men sang quite well and each side clapped and cheered the other.

> I asked a German who sang a solo to sing one of Schumann's songs, so he sang "The Two Grenadiers" spendidly. Our men were a good audience and really enjoyed his singing.[54]

This was followed by the evening burial of German soldiers.

> Then we wished one another good night and a good night's rest, and a Happy Xmas and parted with a salute. I got back to the trench. The Germans sang "*Die Wacht am Rhein*", it sounded well. Then our men sang quite well "Christians Awake", it sounded so well, and with a good night we all got back in our trenches. It was a curious scene, a lovely moonlight night, the German trenches with small lights on them. And the men on both sides gathered in groups on the parapets.
>
> At times we heard the guns in the distance and an occasional rifle shot. I can hear them now, but about us is absolute quiet.[55]

A French officer wrote of singing with his men followed by cries of "*Vive la France!*" and the drinking of champagne:

> At midnight, we held a mass, fifty metres from the Boches, in the trenches. . . . The men sang their carols, carols from their villages, from their childhood . . . carols of peace and gentleness, which coming from these rough lips, seemed more like songs of strife and battle.
>
> Throughout the whole ceremony, the Boches – Bavarian Catholics – did not fire a single shot. For an

> instant the God of goodwill was once more master of this corner of the earth.[56]

Although there are many accounts of German soldiers singing, German troops also reported the singing of others. A member of the Württembergers of the 246th Reserve Regiment of Infantry reported being opposite French troops near Ypres and waiting for the usual "evening blessing" of French artillery fire. But it did not arrive:

> It is possible? Are the French really going to leave us in peace today, Christmas Eve? Then – listen – from across the way came the sound of a festive song. A Frenchman singing a Christmas carol with a marvelous tenor voice. Everyone lay still, listening in the quiet of the night. Is it our imagination or is it maybe meant to lull us into a false sense of security? Or is it in fact the victory of God's love over all human conflict? We all kept on our guard; only our thoughts flew home to our wives and children.[57]

Nearly three-dozen German and English carols, songs, and hymns are written of in soldiers' accounts as having been sung. Cervantes said, "He who sings scares away his woes." Perhaps for at least one night it was true.

The New Year's Day edition of *The Times* published an account from a British major who wrote in a letter home that another unnamed regiment from his own "actually had a football match with the Saxons, who beat them 3-2!!!"[58] It was probably this article that gave the greatest publicity of a holiday game. In 1914, *The Daily Mirror* newspaper published a campaign collecting money to send footballs to British troops, and there is much evidence that footballs were put to good use. Soccer to Americans, but "footer" as the British called it at the time, was extremely popular in both Britain and Germany.

"They [the Saxon regiment] were awfully keen to get up a football match against us; whether it will come off or not, I don't know."[59] Aiden Liddell's Christmas letter to his parents expressing the uncertainty of a forthcoming football match between German and British soldiers contributes to the evidence of whether or not such a contest or contests actually occurred. There were many reports of a game that the Germans won 3-2, but tracking down eyewitnesses and participants is more challenging. However, Kurt Zehmisch of the 134th Saxons recorded in his diary the presence of a real football: "Eventually the English brought a soccer ball from their trenches, and pretty soon a lively game ensued. How marvelously wonderful, yet how strange it was."[60]

There are many British and German reports by soldiers who heard of the game, but fewer who claim to have been present. Yet there are some. Sergeant Bob Lowell of the 3rd London Rifles played and wrote: Even as I write I can scarcely credit what I have seen and done. Indeed it has been a wonderful day."[61]

How likely or feasible would it have been to play a game on a frozen field of shell holes and battle debris? The answer is, "difficult but not impossible." For many soldiers the famed if elusive match is an integral part of the story of the Christmas truce. There are reports of caps being used to mark goals, and, when real balls were unavailable, there were makeshift ones, including tin cans. The sudden Christmas frost had made previously unplayable ground acceptable for sporting skirmishes. A German officer reported a game, perhaps the same one as *The Times* reported: "We marked the goals with our caps. Teams were quickly established for a match on the frozen mud, and the Fritzes beat the Tommies 3-2."[62]

There are also many instances of football being played behind the lines. Private M. Rivett of C Company, Lincolnshire Regiment, wrote to his wife of the short-lived games: "During the day we had football matches with a new ball sent by some kind friends. . . . But what a difference tomorrow! Our battalion will be back in the trenches. Peace and goodwill forgotten. Each man will be trying his best to pick off one or more of the enemy."[63]

Staff Sergeant Clement Barker of the 1st Battalion Grenadier Guards wrote to his brother ". . . a few of our men went out and brought the dead in & buried them (69) & the next thing happened a football kicked out of our trenches & Germans & English played football."[64] A British officer wrote "We had an inter-platoon game of football in the afternoon, a cap comforter stuffed with straw did for the ball, much to the Saxon's amusement."[65] Another wrote: "In the afternoon we even played football between the two lines of trenches, the Germans being interested spectators."[66] Another unit had music and football: "The Scots men started the bagpipes and we had a rare old jollification which included football at which the Germans took part."[67]

While not a football game, there was at least one event that soldiers likened to a football match. The *Daily Mail* published a letter in which the author wrote that after the burial of a Scottish soldier, the chaplain went forward to meet with the German commander and at that moment a rabbit appeared and British and German troops scrambled into No Man's Land in pursuit and "a marvelous thing happened. It was like a football match, the hare being the football, and gray tunicked Germans the one side, and the kilted 'Jocks' the other. The game was won by the Germans, who captured the prize."[68] This then set the stage for fraternization and a temporary peace, with an officer reporting, "a sudden friendship had been struck up, the truce of God had been called, and for the rest of Christmas Day not a shot was fired along our section."[69] It is interesting that the author used the phrase "truce of God." Perhaps he meant it as simply an extension of peace on Christmas Day, or perhaps he was thinking of the centuries-old phrase *Treuga Dei* dating from the eleventh century that designated suspension of fighting on Christian holy days.

The Christmas truce was not the only time footballs appeared on the fields of the Western Front. There are at least two well-documented instances of using football to raise the fighting spirit. The first is of soldiers of the London Irish Rifles passing the ball to each other while advancing toward German lines while under heavy machine gun fire during the 1915 Battle of Loos; a battle with more than 15,000 British casualties.[70] The second was the highly publicized incident of footballs being kicked by British troops across No Man's Land during the first day of the Battle of the Somme (1 July 1916). That was a day that saw the largest number of casualties in British history, with more than 57,000 casualties, of which 19,000 were killed.

If the war and hostilities could have ceased through sports rather than bullets, many would have been glad for it. One British private wrote home: "Several of the Germans were from London and were wishing the war was over. One of them suggested that we should finish it off at football or throwing mud at each other, as we should not get hurt."[71]

Burials and Bullets

For some soldiers the truce was primarily an act of solemnity rather than celebration: its primary purpose was to bury the dead. The sight of unburied soldiers, some mercifully covered by a new snow, diminished the Christmas spirit. At least one soldier intimated, that for his unit, it was indeed the need to bury the dead that initiated interaction between the opposing forces. Private Benjamin Calder wrote to friends at a hometown teashop:

> We were in the trenches of Christmas Day. We spent a merrier day than we expected. There was a truce to bury our dead. We had a short service over the graves, conducted by our minister and the German one. They read the 23rd Psalm and had a short prayer. I don't think I will ever forget the Christmas Day I spent in the trenches. After the service we were speaking to the Germans and getting souvenirs from them.[72]

So also did German soldier Hugo Klemm remember: "So in the grey light of dawn our platoon commander Lieutenant Grosse met an English officer and agreed to bury the dead between the two lines if the higher authorities gave their assent."[73]

A diary from an unidentified soldier in the 2nd Battalion Border Regiment records on 25 December how an officer told his unit "that we were to Bury our Comrades that fell in the Charge on the 18th of Dec. so we all started diging and Burying them side by side and made them a Cross out of the wood of a Biscuit Box and layed them to rest on Xmas day." When the soldiers had been buried, "we all kneled and offered up a Prayer to God above for our Comrades who fell in Honour."[74]

Burials prompted mixed emotions—relief at a pause in the fighting, but sorrow at the loss of comrades. The War Diary of the 2nd Scots Guards recorded a burial service for British soldiers with Germans participating: "The Germans brought the bodies to a halfway line and we buried them. Detachments of British and Germans formed in line and a German and English Chaplain read some prayers alternately."[75] Whereas unit War Diaries normally carried only military facts and assessments, this one goes further: "It was heart-rending to see some of the chaps we knew so well and who had started out in such good spirits on 18 December lying there dead, some with terrible wounds due to the explosive action of the high velocity bullets at short range."[76] Sights of trauma and death were troubling to Germans and British alike. The diary recorded: "Another officer, who could not speak English or French appeared to want to express his feelings, pointed to the dead and reverently said '*Les Braves*'".[77]

A. Pelham-Burn wrote that the joint burial service for the British and German dead that he experienced, some of whom "had been there 6 weeks or more," was very moving. He said: "Our Padre who was up in the trenches for a few hours arranged the prayers and Psalms etc. and then our interpreter wrote them out in German." The funeral service was "then read first in English by our own Padre and then in German by a boy who was studying for the ministry. It was an extraordinary most wonderful sight. The Germans formed up on one side the English on the other the officers standing in front, every head bared."[78]

Many soldiers wrote about the somber burials. Only a few hours after one burial Dr. Frederick George Chandler wrote: "This morning [December 25th] we came across a dead German. We had him buried properly and I got a couple of buttons off the poor devil. A weird Christmas, *n'est-ce pas*?"[79] For many the day was about graves rather than gifts. "We did not fire that day, and everything was so quiet that it seemed like a dream. We took advantage of the quiet day and brought in our dead."[80] Another British soldier's letter stated:

> Between the trenches there were a lot of dead Germans whom we helped bury. In one place where the trenches are only 25 yards apart we could see dead Germans half-buried, their legs and gloved hands sticking out of the ground. The trenches in this position are so close that they are called 'The Death Trap', as hundreds have been killed there.[81]

It is hard to believe that there could be any holiday spirit in such conditions.

A newspaper report from an anonymous colonel of infantry stated that he met in No Man's Land for an hour with troops for a Saxon regiment after which British and Germans participated in a burial service:

> A lot of their dead were lying about in front of our trenches and they thanked us for allowing them to bury. All the German dead were collected and buried and their Captain read a burial service over them in German and in English as many of our men were looking on. At two p.m. he blew a whistle and all the Germans bolted back to their trenches.[82]

The *Daily Mail* carried an account of another joint burial service:

> Dotted over the sixty yards separating the trenches were scores and scores of dead soldiers, and soon spades were flung up by comrades on guard in both trenches, and by instinct each side set to dig graves for their dead. Our padre had seized his chances and found the German commander very ready to agree that after the dead had been buried a short religious service should take place. He told us that the German commander and his officers were as anxious as the British could be to keep Christmas Day as a day of peace.[83]

Writing after Christmas Day, the same writer continued, noting, "(i)t was a memorable sight to see officers and men who had been fighting and as I write are fighting against one another as fiercely as ever, bareheaded, reverent, and keeping sacred truce as they did homage to the memory of the dead on Christmas Day, 1914."[84]

One British officer, not happy at first about the truce wrote:

> The Germans came out, and as soon as we saw they were Saxons I knew it was all right, because they're good fellows on the whole and play the game as far as they know it. The officer came out; we gravely saluted each other, and I then pointed to nine dead Germans lying in midfield and suggested burying them, which both side proceeded to do. We gave them some wooden crosses for them, which completely won them over, and soon the men were on the best of terms and laughing.[85]

Burials on Christmas Day (and other times) were pauses for reflection and prayer. An officer of the Yorkshire Light Infantry was given such pause and reported:

> One wonders, when one sees a German face to face, is this really one of those devils who wrought such devastation—for devastation they have surely wrought. You can hardly believe it, for he seems much the same as other soldiers. I can assure you that there is none of that insensate hatred that one hears about, out here. We are out to kill, and kill we do, at any and every opportunity. But, when all is done and the battle is over, the splendid universal "soldier spirit" comes over all the men, and we cannot help thinking that Kipling must have been in the firing line when he wrote that "East is East and West is West" thing. Just to give you some idea of what I mean, just the other night four German snipers were shot on our wire. The next night our men went out and brought one in who was near and get-at-able and buried him. They did it with just the same

> reverence and sadness as they do with our own dear fellows. I went to look at the grave the next morning, and one of the most uncouth-looking men in my company had placed a cross at the head of the grave, and had written upon it:
>
> "Here lies a German
> We don't know his name,
> He died bravely fighting
> For his Fatherland."
>
> And under that, "got mitt uns" (*sic*), that being the highest effort of all men at German. Not bad for a bloodthirsty Briton, eh? Really that shows the spirit.[86]

Even though the burials were necessary and appropriate, they were also gruesome. A. Pelham-Burns was heartened by the spirit of a joint British-German burial party recovering the dead and called it "a wonderful sight." At the same time, the process was "too awful to describe so I won't attempt it."[87]

Information and Intelligence

Not every participant in the truce viewed it as solely a festivity. A lieutenant in the 2nd Battalion Scots Guards wrote: "They [the Germans] took me for a corporal, a thing I did not discourage, as I had an eye to going as near their lines as possible. I . . .then escorted them back as far as their barbed wire, having a jolly good look round all the time and picking up various little bits of information, which I had not had an opportunity of doing under fire! I went straight to HQ to report."[88]

After experiencing truce, one colonel reported: "These Saxons are the same crowd we have always opposite to us and most of them are quite young, 18-25. Their trenches that our men went into are up to the knee in water so they are far worse off than our men are."[89] The air was also filled with rumors: "They [the Saxon regiment] were quite convinced that the Russians were absolutely beaten, and also the Serbians. Also that they would win, and the war would be over in 6 months."[90]

One officer recorded the festivities of the truce and fraternization, but also wrote:

> I think it did our men good to have a close inspection of their foes; three-quarters of them seemed to be very young youth; I wouldn't mind taking most of them on myself with a bayonet. They said we were very good shots, so I hope by that we've done some damage. They said to the men, "Send us the tip when you're re-

> lieved and we will fire over your heads till then." I don't think![91]

At one location, surprised to see German soldiers in the open and waving their arms to show they were not carrying weapons, kilted soldiers of the 2nd Cameronians were told: "Don't shoot, but count them!"[92]

While many soldiers experienced the truce, it was not universal in the trenches. For some, the war continued with misery and ferocity. One soldier wrote to his parents of a joyless Christmas:

> We came out of the trenches on Christmas night after one of the most miserable times I have ever had; not miserable because I was afraid of the Huns, but wet and cold. . . . Perhaps you read of the conversation on Christmas Day between us and the Germans. It is all lies. The sniping went on just the same; in fact, our captain was wounded, so don't you believe what you see in the papers."[93]

Eighteen months later, on 22 June 1916, the young soldier died and was buried near Ypres in the same cemetery that was the inspiration for the poem of a Canadian medical officer, *In Flanders Fields,* written by Lieutenant-Colonel John McCrae.

Back to Business

Regardless of the hopes and wishes of the troops in the trenches, everyone understood that the truce was temporary. There is no indication that soldiers on either side expected a perpetual peace to result from the truce. A quick end to the war was nowhere in sight. Though they did not know it, the war would continue for another thirty-five months.

Even while it was occurring, not everyone favored the truce. An officer in a Highland regiment expressed frustration that the Germans did not want to fight on Christmas Day.[94]

The truce came to an end at different times on different days depending on where one was serving in the line—but it did come to an end. Sometimes the cease-fires ended unexpectedly from artillery behind the lines shelling enemy trenches and sometimes the truces were ended by pre-arranged signals informally agreed upon by both sides. So it was that a Royal Engineer recorded in his diary that the Germans "threw a message over to say they are going to start firing at midnight and that they take it as an honour to inform us of the fact."[95] Another British soldier wrote that the truce ended "at midnight when one of our officers fired a Very Pistol [flare gun] as signal that time was up, and a volley over their heads."[96]

For most it came to an end too quickly: "Their officers whistled them back after about an hour, and there was a lot of hand shaking and 'Auf Wiedersehens.'... One can hardly realize now, only an hour or so after, that we are all on the lookout, waiting and wondering if they will attack—a thing headquarters rather expect them to do tonight for some reason or other."[97]

On New Year's Eve, Brigadier-General Frederic Heyworth wrote: "Dined with the Gordon Highlanders and danced reels afterwards. The Germans fired at the incoming of the New Year, but up in the air, and we did the same." By the next day, the truce was over for his units. "Our artillery shelled the German trenches and did them a good deal of damage."[98]

By the end of the first week of January 1915, it was all over. What Lieutenant-General Rawlinson called "the fire-swept zone" of No Man's Land was just that once more. For the French it was *le monmansland* and for the Germans, *der Niemansland,* but to be in it meant the same thing for everyone—certain death.

The truce and lack of any major battles or engagements after the middle of December and through New Year's Day provided an opportunity for forces on both sides to reinforce their trenches and resupply their troops. The operational pause also let the soldiers enjoy the flood of holiday parcels and letters that arrived for the war's first Christmas.

Both Germany and Britain made deliberate endeavors to have letters and presents *en masse* sent to their respective troops. German authorities had a policy of sending Christmas trees to every German military unit, including U-boats. Newspapers and magazines in both countries published notices encouraging readers to remember the troops with letters and packages. In Britain, 12 December was announced as the deadline for sending mail to the front for arrival by Christmas and in the six days prior, 250,000 parcels were mailed to France and Belgium. In the following week there were 200,000 more, and throughout the period more than two and a half million letters were mailed to British Tommies. Christmas cards were sent from King George and Queen Mary, and their daughter, Princess Mary, sent every soldier a small brass pocket gift box with tobacco and other amenities.[99] This replicated Queen Victoria's act in 1899 during the Boer War of sending soldiers brass boxes of chocolate. Germans were no less enthusiastic. There was a nationwide campaign to send "*Liebesgaben*"—love gifts—to the front, and Kaiser Wilhelm II, first cousin to King Edward, sent cigars rather than postcards.

The first reports in newspapers about the truce were published within a week and continued through the third week in January. Some credit the *New York Times* with being the first to break the story of the truce. The 31 December 1914 edition carried a "Special Cable" from "Northern France" with a heading of "Foes in the Trenches Swap Pies for Wine" and also published a widely printed letter from "an officer in the Queen's Westminster Rifles" under a heading of "Fraternizing Between the Lines." Soon after, there were letters printed in other newspapers in the United States such as the Philadelphia *Evening Public Ledger* (04 January 1915, Night Extra).

From 31 December 1914 until 20 January 1915, there were more than sixty reports of the truce published in the major British newspapers the *Daily Mail, Daily Telegraph, Morning Post, Manchester Guardian,* and *The Times.* However, there were no official communications about the event published, and only a couple of editorials attempted to situate the truce in the larger war narrative. Apart from brief introductions to the letters, newspapers offered no commentary on the truce and gave no official information on it. Those who penned the letters spoke for themselves without editorial censorship.[100]

By the third week of January, published personal accounts by those who participated in the truce dwindled considerably. What were reported in the British newspapers were the responses of the French and German military authorities to the unofficial ceasefires. Newspaper accounts also made distinctions between Saxon units, seen as more humane and similar to British forces, and Prussian units that were viewed as more militaristic. The 9 January 1915 edition of the popular weekly *Illustrated London News* carried a cover story of the truce wherein columnist Charles Lowe wrote: "Christmastide brought with it to our trenches in Flanders a sort of 'truce of God' by mutual consent, accompanied by such fraternizing between opposing foes as had never been seen, perhaps, since Peninsular days or the siege of Sebastopol."[101] The reports of the truce were as complex as the true experiences, and the printed letters show that the press was willing to report the diverse accounts and opinions.

Not every report from the front during the holiday season was of the truce. On 31 December, *The Times* printed a letter under the headline "Artillerymen's Christmas," that reported some pause in hostilities but also stated, "all Christmas Eve, a steady ripple of sniping runs along the trenches, and every time I wake in the night I hear it."[102] The printed letter of one British soldier showed that he had no expectation that the Christmas truce would lead to any larger armistice: "I don't expect we shall shake hands with the enemy again for a long time to come."[103] Regrettably, he was correct.

Weeks before Christmas, shortly after the war erupted, the newly-elected pontiff in Rome, Pope Benedict XV, had published a plea for peace, but it was rebuffed by all. One publication, American weekly *The New Republic*, retorted from the neutral United States: "If men must hate, it is perhaps just as well that they make no Christmas truce."[104] It stated: "The stench of battle should rise above the churches where they preach good-will to men. A few carols, a little incense and some tinsel will heal no wounds."[105] Even a resolution introduced in the U.S. Senate urging a twenty-five day Christmas truce had come to naught.[106]

Even if the pontiff's plea for peace had been accepted in France and Flanders, peace was unlikely to occur elsewhere. On the Eastern Front, Christmas for Orthodox Churches fell on 7 January, not 25 December. In the Middle East, where Islamic Turkey was aligned and fighting alongside Germany and the other Central Powers, Christmas meant little. Similarly, Christmas meant little for Japanese who were fighting with the Allies.[107]

Beyond the battlefield, the lack of an official truce provided a glimpse of what was occurring intellectually across Europe. Nineteenth-century theology (and art, music, and literature) died on the battlefields of France. The mantras of the "brotherhood of man" and "every day in every way the world is getting better and better" were drowned out by millions and millions of artillery shells and the cries and screams of the wounded and dying.

Some British military leaders were concerned that Germany might use Christmas as a day of attack. Late on 24 December a signal was issued to all units stating: "It is thought that the enemy may be contemplating an attack during Christmas or New Year. Special vigilance will be maintained during this period."[108] By the time it belatedly reached the front, unofficial truce was underway. On 26 December, after a visit to the front, General Sir Horace Smith-Dorrien wrote: "I was shown a report from one section of how, on Christmas Day, a friendly gathering had taken place on the neutral ground between the trenches, recounting that many officers had taken part in it.... To finish this war quickly, we must keep up the fighting spirit and do all we can to discourage friendly intercourse."[109]

Similar sentiments were expressed by Captain Sir Morgan Crofton, of the 2nd Life Guards, Cavalry Division, who wrote in his diary on 4 January 1915 blaming the press for reporting the truce:

> The London papers have been full of accounts of the last week or so of regiments of German infantry fraternizing with our troops on Xmas Day. Apparently the Queen's Westminsters did, but from many quarters there are the same reports of German and English soldiers mixing, shaking hands, exchanging cigars and cigarettes, even taking photos of each other. This is all very well but *ce n'est pas la guerre.*
>
> Boshy papers of the halfpenny type slobber over

> this rubbish, but everyone out here condemns it. This is WAR, bloody War, and not a mother's meeting.[110]

Even though some condemned the truce, many did not, including some of the more senior ones such as Lieutenant General Sir Henry Rawlinson, who wrote in his personal diary on 27 December of the event, stating he was "rather suspicious of them [Germans]," but he did not express displeasure with the truce.[111]

Widely reported in the British press, the truce was largely ignored by German newspapers, and French ones denied French participation, stating that French soldiers shouted, "Shut up German pigs!" as soon as German soldiers began singing. However, some French units did participate, as did a few Belgians.[112] A French soldier writing home after the truce told his mother that, while meeting in No Man's Land, soldiers chorused in their own language, "*Y bas la guerre!*"—"Down with the war!" Carl Mühlegg of the 17th Bavarian Regiment remembered shouting, "*Nie wieder Krieg! Das walte Gott!*"—"No more war! It's what God wants!"[113]

Earlier, Mühlegg had been sent to the rear area supply depot to pick up the unit's *Weihnachtsbäume* (Christmas tree). After returning under fire, he handed the thirty-two inch tree to his captain. "I handed the captain the little Christmas tree. . . . He lit the candles and wished his soldiers, the German nation and the whole world 'Peace according to the message from the angel.'" When near midnight the soldiers met the enemy in No Man's Land,

Mühlegg wrote: "Never was I as keenly aware of the insanity of war."[114]

Even those not directly participating in the truce at the trenches could not help but be affected by the fact that it was Christmas in time of war. Katherine Luard, a nurse serving just behind the lines, had been one of the first British nurses sent to France at the outbreak of the war. Previously, she had served two years in South Africa during the Boer War. She published her diary anonymously in 1915 as *Diary of a Nursing Sister on the Western Front.* On Christmas Eve and Christmas Day she was on an ambulance train traveling to the town of Merville. Each day she worked on trains that were moving wounded from casualty clearing stations back to base hospitals at the Channel ports. In part, on Christmas Eve she recorded:

> There are two men (only one is a boy) on the train who got wounded on Monday night (both compound fracture of the thigh) and were only taken out of the trench this morning, Thursday, to a Dressing Station and then straight on to our train. (We heard the guns this morning.) Why they are alive I don't know, but I'm afraid they won't live long: they are sunken and grey-faced and just strong enough to say, "Anyway, I'm out of the trench now." They had drinks of water now and then in the field but no dressings, and lay in the slush. Stretcher-bearers are shot down immediately, with or without the wounded, by German snipers. And this is Christmas, and the world is supposed to be civilized.[115]

Many of the troops she nursed on Christmas Eve were Indian serving in the Indian Cavalry Corps. They were far from home and unused to the European winter weather. Even though they were Hindu, Christmas cards were given to them in the spirit of the season:

> The Indians each had one, and salaamed and said, "God save you," and "I will pray to God for you," and "God win your enemies," and "God kill many Germans," and "The Indian men too cold, kill more Germans if not too cold." One with a S.A. ribbon spotted mine and said, "Africa same like you."[116]

For Nurse Luard, Christmas Eve turned to Christmas Day before she finished duty after midnight and wrote: "Just unloaded, going to turn in; we are off again at 5 A.M. tomorrow."[117]

Christmas Day brought Nurse Luard no relief from work. On the train she wrote:

> 11 A.M. Sharp white frost, fog becoming denser as we get nearer to Belgium. . . . 12 *Midnight.*—Still on the road. . . . We are wondering what the chances are of getting to bed to-night. . . . 4 A.M.—Very late in getting in to B.; not unloading till morning. Just going to turn in now till breakfast time. End of Xmas Day.[118]

Nurse Luard also wrote of packages and letters from home, including the Princess Mary gift tins. Like ripples from rocks tossed into a pond, the war in the trenches touched everyone all the way back to the towns at home. As one newspaper reported: "It was a day of peace in war. It is only a pity that it was not a decisive peace."[119]

Memory and Meaning

So what does it all mean? Did it really occur, or was it just another war myth infused with religious sentimentality like the stories of the "Angel of Mons" or the "White Comrade?" Was the truce simply a day or few days respite for war-weary troops, or was there something more significant in the event? Is it simply to be seen as a postscript in an account of a long and brutal war? In the weeks, months, and years after the truce, it was largely seen as just that—curious and even understandable, but insignificant. Truces during times of war are not unusual. The story of this truce is not a legend, but it is legendary. It truly did occur, and it was "the culminating episode of a dramatic and tragic year."[120]

Two of the prevailing myths of the truce are that the newspapers suppressed accounts of it and that participants were reprimanded. Neither is correct. Within a week of the event the press was publishing letters about it, and the British had no official reprimand for any of the participants, and no one was court-martialed.[121] The press may not have known where to place the truce in the contemporary war narrative, but it was not avoided.

A third myth is that British authorities did not acknowledge the truce. However, official unit diaries and records show otherwise. One example is the report of the commanding officer of the 1st Royal Irish Rifles, who wrote of "this curious situation—'a soldiers' truce.'"[122] Some unit diaries mentioned it only briefly, but others gave extensive details. Yet, the richest source of information remains the letters sent by the soldiers.

Prolific author, historian and politician John Buchan, who served in the war and was a staff officer for Field Marshall Douglas Haig, believed that the truce occurred because it was practical and was probably "connived at by the commanders on both sides, for some of our trenches were nearly flooded out, and the Germans had much timbering to do."[123]

In the years following the war, historians and politicians said little of the truce. Like so much in war, it was remembered mainly by those who experienced it. In 1962, veteran author and poet Robert Graves published a short story about the truce but with a pessimistic interpretation of what it meant for future generations. Since the 1960s, the truce has resurfaced as part of larger interpretations of the futility and senselessness of the war. It has also been depicted in films such as *Joyeux Noël* (2005) and in music such as John McCutcheon's moving song "Christmas in the Trenches" (1984).[124]

For centuries, warring armies have paused during conflict to allow removal of the dead and wounded from battlefields or to observe cultural celebrations or religious holy days. What distinguished 1914 Christmas truce was that it was unofficial rather than official; it originated from the trenches rather than from headquarters. Indeed, there were senior military leaders who disapproved of the truce because they feared that it would weaken the will to fight. They may have been correct.

Historians of the First World War have viewed the truce in various ways, typically in ones that correspond to their larger interpretations of the meaning of the war. Sometimes their accounts of the truce are accurate, other times, less so.[125] Some see it as a minor postscript and human-interest story. Others understand it as the first visible reaction to the emerging needless slaughter of a generation. Yet others view the event as a series of spontaneous acts of pacifism or see in it irony that at the same time prayers for victory and defeat of the enemy were being said in churches of Britain and Germany, soldiers were exchanging mementos and cigarettes in No Man's Land.

From a broader perspective, a few writers have attempted to evaluate the truce against the backdrop of the entire war. Christmas truce historian Stanley Weintraub writes that it has a symbolism that exceeds the chronological boundaries of the war and that "the end of the war and the failure of the peace would validate the Christmas cease-fire as the only meaningful episode in the apocalypse."[126] Weintraub's words reflect some of the sentiment expressed at the time of the war. Sir Arthur Conan Doyle, the creator of Sherlock Holmes, and a father who later lost his son in the war, described the Christmas truce as "one human episode amid all the atrocities which have stained the memory of the war."[127]

Some authors have reflected upon the event in an attempt to understand its broader social and historical significance. Paul Fussell, author of the landmark study *The*

Great War and Modern Memory (1975), wrote:

> The Christmas truce was the last twitch of the 19th century. By that I mean it was the last public moment in which it was assumed that people were nice, and that the Dickens view of the world was a credible view. . . . It's the last gesture of the 19th century idea that human beings are getting better the longer the human race goes on. Nobody could believe that after the First World War, and certainly not after the Second.[128]

Peter Simkins, former Senior Historian at the Imperial War Museum, also views the truce in the context of changing eras:

> It is very much a 1914 phenomenon. I think it's wrapped up with the fact that you could still be sentimental in 1914. Whereas, when total war became much more all pervasive later in the war, and the war became a much more sort of mass war for everybody, I think the sort of slightly old-fashioned sentiments lost their place and it became a much nastier business.[129]

There is much to be said for these words. The truce occurred before the deployment of mustard gas and the battles of Verdun, the Somme, and Gallipoli. It was a symbol of the human spirit not yet crushed by the force of mechanized and chemical warfare. It was a small peace in a big war.

For the remainder of the war there were a few small-scale truces that occurred during holiday seasons, holy days such as Easter, and for other reasons, but such pauses were discouraged and terminated by orders from senior officers.

Historian Niall Ferguson has written: "The First World War was something worse than a tragedy, which is something we are taught by the theatre to regard as ultimately unavoidable. It was nothing less than the greatest *error* of modern history."[130] He is right. By the time the guns fell silent in November 1918, more than nine million soldiers had died—an average of six thousand a day every day for the four years of the war.

When the war began, British Foreign Secretary Sir Edward Grey famously remarked to a friend: "The lamps are going out all over Europe, we shall not see them lit again in our life-time." For the millions who perished in the war, many before the Christmas truce, his statement was true. Historian Malcolm Brown writes of the truce: "It never could have stopped the war." He is correct, but he is also right in observing: "In a time of deep darkness it lit a candle of hope."[131]

It has now been more than a century since the Christmas truce. "Peace on earth" still eludes humanity. It is a hope but not a reality. While some will say that nothing good ever comes out of war, the Christmas truce as experienced by thousands of soldiers and remembered by later generations stands as a reminder that such a perspective is not entirely true.

In December 1918, four years after the 1914 Christmas truce, there was no need for another one. The Great War had come to an end a month earlier at the eleventh hour of the eleventh day of the eleventh month. That peace however, was short-lived and a generation later young men would again be marching to war. The Christmas truce would not be repeated. Trees would not be lit and troops would not sing as they had on Christmas Eve in 1914, "The hopes and fears of all the years are met in thee tonight." The words were still true, but few were listening.

Notes

1. Dorothy Hoobler and Thomas Hoobler, *The Trenches: Fighting on the Western Front in World War I* (New York: G. P. Putnam's Sons, 1978), 33.

2. Winston S. Churchill to H. H. Asquith, 29 December 191, cited in Richard Langworth, ed. *Churchill by Himself: The Definitive Collection of Quotations* (New York: PublicAffairs, 2008), 35.

3. Cited in Stanley Weintraub, *Silent Night: The Story of the World War I Christmas Truce* (New York: The Free Press, 2001), 43.

4. Malcolm Brown and Shirley Seaton, *Christmas Truce: The Western Front December 1914* (London: Pan Books, 1996), 45, 56.

5. Weintraub, *Silent Night*, 8-9.

6. W. B. P. Spencer, 25 December 1914 letter cited in Theresa Blom Crocker, "'A Remarkable Instance': The Christmas Truce and Its Role in the Contemporaneous Narrative of the First World War," Unpublished M.A. Thesis. Lexington: University of Kentucky, 2012, 44.

7. Cited in Alan Cleaver, Lesley Park, et al. *Not a Shot was Fired: Letters from the Christmas Truce 1914*, 2nd ed. (Raliegh: Lulu Books, 2008), 20.

8. Cited in Cleaver, Park, et al. *Not a Shot was Fired*,18.

9. Dorothy Hoobler and Thomas Hoobler, *The Trenches: Fighting on the Western Front in World War I* (New York: G. P. Putnam's Sons, 1978), 32.

10. C. S. Lewis, *Surprised by Joy: The Shape of My Early Life* (London: Geoffrey Bles, 1955), 184.

11. A. D. Chater, 13 January 1915 letter, Imperial War Museum Collection No. 1697.

12. Cited in Brown and Seaton, *Christmas Truce*, 26.

13. Lance-Corporal Henderson, Royal Engineers letter reprinted in *The Hampshire Chronicle*, cited in Cleaver, Park, et al. *Not a Shot was Fired*, 24.

14. Cited in Malcolm Brown, "The Christmas Truce 1914: The British Story," in Marco Ferro, et al, *Meetings in No Man's Land: Christmas 1914 and Fraternization in the Great War* (London: Constable & Robinson, 2007), 18-19.

15. "Burrowing to Berlin: The Work of Spades and Picks," *The Independent*, 8 March 1915, 357.

16. "Burrowing to Berlin: The Work of Spades and Picks," *The Independent*, 8 March 1915, 357.

17. J. Selby Grigg, 26 December 1914 letter, Imperial War Museum Collection No. 3881.

18. Cited in Weintraub, *Silent Night*, 45.

19. Cited in Weintraub, *Silent Night*, 45.

20. Weintraub, *Silent Night*, 51.

21. Corporal Leon Harris, 13th Battalion London Regiment (Kensington) letter to his parents reprinted in *The Exeter Express and Echo*, cited in Cleaver, Park, et al. *Not a Shot was Fired*, 21.

22. Frederick George Chandler, letter to sister, 25 December 1914, cited in "War letters home: 'The Christmas truce saw German soldiers sharing a barrel of beer with us British'" at http://www.telegraph.co.uk/history/world-war-one/inside-first-world-war/part-four (accessed 8 August 2014).

23. Cited in Cleaver, Park, et al. *Not a Shot was Fired*, 20.

24. Peter Simkins, "The Christmas Truce—A Mutual Curiosity," at http://www.pbs.org/greatwar/historian/hist_simkins_04_truce.html (accessed 21 August 2014).

25. M. Holroyd, December 31 1914 letter, Imperial War Museum Collection No. 7364 cited in cited in Crocker, "'A Re-

markable Instance': The Christmas Truce and Its Role in the Contemporaneous Narrative of the First World War," 45.

26. Corporal Leon Harris, 13th Battalion London Regiment (Kensington) letter to his parents reprinted in *The Exeter Express and Echo,* cited in Cleaver, Park, et al. *Not a Shot was Fired*, 21.

27. Chandler, letter to sister, 25 December 1914, cited in "War letters home: 'The Christmas truce saw German soldiers sharing a barrel of beer with us British'" at http://www.telegraph.co.uk/history/world-war-one/inside-first-world-war/part-four (accessed 8 August 2014).

28. Lance Corporal Cooper letter published in *The Bedfordshire Times and Independent*, cited in Cleaver, Park, et al. *Not a Shot was Fired*, 18.

29. Rifleman J. Reading, published in *The Bucks Examiner*, cited in Cleaver, Park, et al. *Not a Shot was Fired*,19.

30. Anonymous private quoted in *The Whitehaven News*, cited in Cleaver, Park, et al. *Not a Shot was Fired*, 20.

31. Aiden Liddell 25 December 1914 letter to parents published in *The Hants and Berks Gazette*, cited in Cleaver, Lesley, et al. *Not a Shot was Fired*, 22.

32. Rifleman C. H. Brazier, Queen's Westminsters of Bishops Stortford letter printed in *The Hertfordshire Mercury*, cited in Cleaver, Park, et al. *Not a Shot was Fired*, 30-31.

33. Anonymous private quoted in *The Whitehaven News*, cited in Cleaver, Park, et al. *Not a Shot was Fired*, 20.

34. *Daily Telegraph* telegram from Rotterdam reprinted in *The Staffordshire Sentinel* on 04 January 1915, cited in Cleaver, Park, et al. *Not a Shot was Fired*, 59.

35. C. G. V. Wellesley, December 25 1914 letter, Imperial War Museum Collection No. 15579, cited in Crocker, "'A Remarkable Instance': The Christmas Truce and Its Role in the Contemporaneous Narrative of the First World War," 50.

36. H. J. Chappell, December 27 1914 letter, cited in Crocker, "'A Remarkable Instance': The Christmas Truce and Its Role in the Contemporaneous Narrative of the First World War," 50.

37. W. H. Diggle, December 27 1914 letter, cited in Crocker, "'A Remarkable Instance': The Christmas Truce and Its Role in the Contemporaneous Narrative of the First World War," 51.

38. Lance-Corporal Henderson, Royal Engineers, letter printed in *The Hampshire Chronicle*, cited in Cleaver, Park, et al. *Not a Shot was Fired*, 23.

39. Lance-Corporal Henderson, Royal Engineers, letter printed in *The Hampshire Chronicle*, cited in Cleaver, Park, et al. *Not a Shot was Fired*, 27-28.

40. Cited in "Burrowing to Berlin: The Work of Spades and Picks," *The Independent*, 8 March 1915, 357.

41. Cited in "Burrowing to Berlin: The Work of Spades and Picks," *The Independent*, 8 March 1915, 357.

42. Cited in Brown and Seaton, *Christmas Truce*, 154.

43. Cited in Cleaver, Park, et al. *Not a Shot was Fired*, 20.

44. Chandler, letter to sister, 25 December 1914, cited in "War letters home: 'The Christmas truce saw German soldiers sharing a barrel of beer with us British'" at http://www.telegraph.co.uk/history/world-war-one/inside-first-world-war/part-four (accessed 8 August 2014).

45. Cited in "Burrowing to Berlin: The Work of Spades and Picks," *The Independent*, 8 March 1915, 357.

46. Brown, "The Christmas Truce 1914: The British Story, "in Ferro, et al, *Meetings in No Man's Land*, 19.

47. Andrew Hamilton and Alan Reed eds., *Meet at Dawn, Unarmed: Captain Robert Hamilton's Account of Trench Warfare and the Christmas Truce in 1914* (Walton, Warwick, UK: Dene House, 2009), 112.

48. Hamilton and Alan Reed eds., *Meet at Dawn, Unarmed*, 20.

49. Cited in Brown, "The Christmas Truce 1914: The British Story, " in Ferro, et al, *Meetings in No Man's Land*, 43.

50. Lance-Corporal Henderson, Royal Engineers letter reprinted in *The Hampshire Chronicle,* cited in Cleaver, Park, et al. *Not a Shot was Fired*, 24.

51. Cited in Brown, "The Christmas Truce 1914: The British Story, " in Ferro, et al, *Meetings in No Man's Land*, 29.

52. Cited in Brown, "The Christmas Truce 1914: The British Story," in Ferro, et al, *Meetings in No Man's Land*, 29.

53. Cited in Brown, "The Christmas Truce 1914: The British Story," in Ferro, et al, *Meetings in No Man's Land*, 30.

54. Cited in Brown, "The Christmas Truce 1914: The British Story," in Ferro, et al, *Meetings in No Man's Land*, 30.

55. Cited in Brown, "The Christmas Truce 1914: The British Story," in Ferro, et al, *Meetings in No Man's Land*, 31-32.

56. Cited in Brown and Seaton, *Christmas Truce*, 73.

57. Cited in Brown and Seaton, *Christmas Truce*, 73.

58. *The Times,* "Letters from the Front," 01 January 1915.

59. Aiden Liddell 25 December 1914 letter to parents published in *The Hants and Berks Gazette,* cited in Cleaver, Park, et al. *Not a Shot was Fired*, 22.

60. Cited in Weintraub, *Silent Night*, 105.

61. Cited in Weintraub, *Silent Night*, 105.

62. Cited in Brown, "The Christmas Truce 1914: The British Story," in Ferro, et al, *Meetings in No Man's Land*, 45.

63. M. Rivett, 25 December 1914 letter to wife reprinted in *The Grimsby Daily Telegraph*, cited in Cleaver, Park, et al. *Not a Shot was Fired*, 60.

64. http://www.dailymail.co.uk/news/article-2252454/A-foot-

ball-kicked-trenches-played-Germans-Previously-unseen-letter-Clement-Barker-recounting-World-War-One-Christmas-Day-truce-1914-revealed.html (accessed 12 October 2014).

65. Cited in "Burrowing to Berlin: The Work of Spades and Picks," *The Independent,* 8 March 1915, 357.

66. Rifleman Smith letter home reprinted in *The Warwick and Warwickshire Advertiser*, cited in Cleaver, Park, et al. *Not a Shot was Fired*, 61.

67. Clement Barker, 29 December 1914 letter to brother cited in "Silent night: goalie night" by Euan Stretch, Mirror, 24 December 2012 at http://www.mirror.co.uk/news/uk-news/letter-tells-of-world-war-one-1504190 (accessed 12 October 2014).

68. The *Daily Mail,* "One Day of Peace at the Front," 01 January 1915.

69. The *Daily Mail,* "One Day of Peace at the Front," 01 January 1915.

70. "Football kicked in No Man's Land in First World War is saved," *Metro,* 11 March 2011 at http://metro.co.uk/2011/03/11/football-kicked-in-no-mans-land-in-first-world-war-is-saved-643812/ (accessed 10 October 2014).

71. Private Simnet of 1st North Staffordshire Regiment letter to father reprinted in *The Staffordshire Sentinel* cited in Cleaver, Park, et al. *Not a Shot was Fired*, 58.

72. Benjamin Calder letter published in the *Bedfordshire Times,* January 1915 cited in Cleaver, Park, et al. *Not a Shot was Fired,* 84.

73. Cited in Weintraub, *Silent Night,* 57.

74. Unknown soldier, 25 December 25 1914 diary entry, Imperial War Museum No. 8631, cited in Croker, "'A Remarkable Instance': The Christmas Truce and Its Role in the Contemporaneous Narrative of the First World War," 49.

75. Cited in Brown, "The Christmas Truce 1914: The British Story," in Ferro, et al, *Meetings in No Man's Land*, 33.

76. Cited in Brown, "The Christmas Truce 1914: The British Story," in Ferro, et al, *Meetings in No Man's Land*, 34.

77. Cited in Brown, "The Christmas Truce 1914: The British Story," in Ferro, et al, *Meetings in No Man's Land*, 34.

78. A. Pelham-Burns, undated letter, cited in Croker, "'A Remarkable Instance': The Christmas Truce and Its Role in the Contemporaneous Narrative of the First World War," 49-50.

79. Chandler, letter to sister, 25 December 1914, cited in "War letters home: 'The Christmas truce saw German soldiers sharing a barrel of beer with us British'" at http://www.telegraph.co.uk/history/world-war-one/inside-first-world-war/part-four (accessed 8 August 2014).

80. Rifleman J. Reading, published in *The Bucks Examiner*, cited in Cleaver, Park, et al. *Not a Shot was Fired*, 19.

81. Letter printed in *The Hertfordshire Mercury*, cited in Cleaver, Park, et al. *Not a Shot was Fired*, 31.

82. Anonymous report in *The Grimsby Daily Telegraph*, cited in Cleaver, Park, et al. *Not a Shot was Fired*, 59.

83. The *Daily Mail*, "One Day of Peace at the Front," 01 January 1915.

84. The *Daily Mail*, "One Day of Peace at the Front," 01 January 1915.

85. Cited in "Burrowing to Berlin: The Work of Spades and Picks," *The Independent*, 8 March 1915, 357.

86. Cited in "Burrowing to Berlin: The Work of Spades and Picks," *The Independent*, 8 March 1915, 356-57. The reference to Kipling comes from his poem "The Ballad of East and West" (1889).

87. A. Pelham-Burns, undated letter. Cited in Croker, "'A Re-

markable Instance': The Christmas Truce and Its Role in the Contemporaneous Narrative of the First World War," 49-50.

88. Cited in "The Christmas Truce of 1914," at http://www.world war1.com/heritage/xmast.htm (accessed 21 Aug 2014).

89. Anonymous report in *The Grimsby Daily Telegraph*, cited in Cleaver, Park, et al. *Not a Shot was Fired*, 59.

90. Aiden Liddell, 25 December 1914 letter to parents published in *The Hants and Berks Gazette*, cited in Cleaver, Park, et al. *Not a Shot was Fired*, 22.

91. Cited in "Burrowing to Berlin: The Work of Spades and Picks," *The Independent*, 8 March 1915, 357.

92. Cited in Weintraub, *Silent Night*,14.

93. Pat Collard, letter to parents cited in Cleaver, Park, et al. *Not a Shot was Fired*, 51, 52, 53.

94. *The Times*, "Letters from the Front/More Tales of the Truce/ Christmas Goodwill/Friendly Meetings with the Enemy," 2 January 1915.

95. J. Fenton, 27 December 1915 diary entry, Imperial War Museum Collection No. 12033. Cited in Croker, "'A Remarkable Instance': The Christmas Truce and Its Role in the Contemporaneous Narrative of the First World War," 54.

96. J. Wedderburn-Maxwell, 26 December 1914 letter, cited in Crocker, "'A Remarkable Instance': The Christmas Truce and Its Role in the Contemporaneous Narrative of the First World War," 54-55.

97. Aiden Liddell, 25 December 1914 letter to parents published in *The Hants and Berks Gazette*, cited in Cleaver, Park, et al. *Not a Shot was Fired*, 22.

98. Cited in Brown, "The Christmas Truce 1914: The British Story, "in Ferro, et al, *Meetings in No Man's Land*, 61.

99. Brown, "The Christmas Truce 1914: The British Story," in

Ferro, et al, *Meetings in No Man's Land*, 23-24. There were boxes for smokers and nonsmokers as well as special boxes for Indian troops. See also, Jeremy Archer, *A Royal Christmas* (London: Elliott and Thompson Limited, 2012), 237-47 and Stanley Weintraub, *Silent Night*, 9-12.

100. Crocker, "'A Remarkable Instance': The Christmas Truce and Its Role in the Contemporaneous Narrative of the First World War," 61-62, 68.

101. *Illustrated London News*, "The Great War," 09 January 1915.

102. *The Times*, "Letters from the Front/Christmas Truce/Football with the Enemy," 31 December 1914 cited in Crocker, "'A Remarkable Instance': The Christmas Truce and Its Role in the Contemporaneous Narrative of the First World War," 68.

103. *Daily Telegraph*, "Sorry to Fight Us," 02 January 1915.

104. Cited in Stanley Weintraub, *Silent Night*, xvi.

105. Cited in Stanley Weintraub, xvi.

106. Weintraub, *Silent Night*, xvi.

107. Weintraub, *Silent Night*, xvi.

108. Cited in Brown, "The Christmas Truce 1914: The British Story," in Ferro, et al, *Meetings in No Man's Land*, 26.

109. Cited in Brown, "The Christmas Truce 1914: The British Story," in Ferro, et al, *Meetings in No Man's Land*, 51.

110. Cited in Brown, "The Christmas Truce 1914: The British Story," in Ferro, et al, *Meetings in No Man's Land*, 56.

111. Cited in Brown, "The Christmas Truce 1914: The British Story," in Ferro, et al, *Meetings in No Man's Land*, 56.

112. See Weintraub, *Silent Night*, 23, 40-47, 65-69.

113. Cited inWeintraub, *Silent Night*, 32.

114. Cited in Weintraub, *Silent Night*, 33.

115. Anonymous, *Diary of a Nursing Sister on the Western Front 1914-1915* (Edinburgh and London: William Blackwood and Sons, 1915), from http://www.gutenberg.org/files/18910/18910-h.htm (accessed 16 October 2012).

116. Anonymous, *Diary of a Nursing Sister on the Western Front 1914-1915*, n.p. [electronic edition]. Although it was a Christian holiday, soldiers of other faiths (and not faith), experienced and wrote of the truce. See for example the responses of Jewish soldiers and poets in Peter C. Appelbaum, *Loyal Sons: Jewish Soldiers in the German Army in the Great War*. London: Vallentine Mitchell, 2014.

117. Anonymous, *Diary of a Nursing Sister on the Western Front 1914-1915*, n.p. [electronic edition].

118. Anonymous, *Diary of a Nursing Sister on the Western Front 1914-1915*, n.p. [electronic edition].

119. *Daily Telegraph* telegram from Rotterdam reprinted in *The Staffordshire Sentinel* on 04 January 1915, cited in Cleaver, Park, et al. *Not a Shot was Fired*, 59.

120. Brown and Seaton, *Christmas Truce*, 1.

121. Crocker, "'A Remarkable Instance': The Christmas Truce and Its Role in the Contemporaneous Narrative of the First World War," 89.

122. Brown, "The Christmas Truce 1914: The British Story," in Ferro, et al, *Meetings in No Man's Land*, 23-24.

123. John Buchan, *Nelson's History of the War: Volume V* (London: Thomas Nelson and Sons, 1915), 39.

124. See Crocker, "'A Remarkable Instance': The Christmas Truce and Its Role in the Contemporaneous Narrative of the First World War," 93-101 for further discussion.

125. See for example, Crocker's analysis of John Keegan's account in her thesis, p. 10, fn. 11 noting eleven inaccuracies in

his brief paragraph regarding the truce. What this shows in part is the enormous amount of material, sometimes undocumented and conflicting, with which historians must work.

126. Weintraub, *Silent Night*, xvi.

127. Cited in "War letters home: 'The Christmas truce saw German soldiers sharing a barrel of beer with us British'" at http://www.telegraph.co.uk/history/world-war-one/inside-first-world-war/part-four (accessed 8 August 2014).

128. Paul Fussell, "The Christmas Tree [sic]—The Last Twitch" at http://www.pbs.org/greatwar/historian/hist_fussell_04_xmas.html (accessed 8 August 2014).

129. Peter Simkins, "The Christmas Truce—A Mutual Curiosity," at http://www.pbs.org/greatwar/historian/hist_simkins_04_truce.html (accessed 21 August 2014).

130. Niall Ferguson, *The Pity of War: Explaining World War I* (London: Allan Lane, 1998), 462.

131. Brown, "The Christmas Truce 1914: The British Story," in Ferro, et al, *Meetings in No Man's Land*, 77.

Recommend Reading

Anonymous [Katherine Luard]. *Diary of a Nursing Sister on the Western Front 1914-1915*. Edinburgh and London: William Blackwood and Sons, 1915.

Appelbaum, Peter C. *Loyal Sons: Jewish Soldiers and the Great War.* London: Vallentine Mitchell, 2014.

Archer, Jeremy, *A Royal Christmas.* London: Elliot and Thompson Limited, 2012.

Baker, Chris. *The Truce: The Day the War Stopped.* Stroud: Amberly Publishing, 2014.

Brown, Malcolm. *The Imperial War Museum Book of 1914: The Men Who Went to War.* London: Sidgwick and Jackson, 2004.

Brown, Malcolm and Shirley Seaton. *Christmas Truce: The Western Front December 1914.* London: Pan Books, 1996.

Cleaver, Alan and Lesley Park, et al. *Not a Shot was Fired: Letters from the Christmas Truce 1914*, 2nd ed. Raliegh: Lulu Books, 2008.

Crocker, Theresa Blom. *The Christmas Truce: Myth, Memory, and the First World War.* Lexington: The University of Kentucky Press, 2015.

Crocker, Theresa Blom. "'A Remarkable Instance': The Christmas Truce and Its Role in the Contemporaneous Narrative of the First World War," Unpublished M.A. Thesis. Lexington: The University of Kentucky, 2012.

Ellis, John. *Eye-Deep in Hell: Trench Warfare in World War I.* Baltimore: The Johns Hopkins University Press, 1976.

Ferguson, Niall. *The Pity of War: Explaining World War One.* London: Allan Lane, 1998.

Ferro, Marco et al. *Meetings in No Man's Land: Christmas 1914 and Fraternization in the Great War.* London: Constable & Robinson, 2007.

Fussell, Paul. *The Great War and Modern Memory.* New York: Oxford University Press, 1975.

Hamilton, Andrew and Alan Reed, ed. *Meet at Dawn, Unarmed: Captain Robert Hamilton's Account of Trench Warfare and the Christmas Truce in 1914.* Walton, Warwick: Dene House Publishing, 2009.

Hastings, Max. Catastrophe: *Europe Goes to War 1914.* London: William Collins, 2013.

Hoobler, Dorothy and Thomas Hoobler, *The Trenches: Fighting on the Western Front in World War I.* New York: G. P. Putnam's Sons, 1978.

Holmes, Richard. *Tommy: The British Soldier on the Western Front 1914-18.* London: HarperCollins, 2004.

Jürgs, Michael. *Der kleine Frieden im Großen Krieg, Westfront 1914: Als Deutsche, Franzosen und Briten gemeinsam Weihnachten feirerten.* München: C. Bertelsmann Verlag, 2003.

Langworth, Richard, ed. *Churchill by Himself: The Definitive Collection of Quotations.* New York: PublicAffairs, 2008.

Meyer, G. J. *A World Undone: The Story of the Great War 1914 to 1918.* New York: Delacorte Press, 2006.

Richards, Anthony. *The True Story of the Christmas Truce: British and German Eyewitness Accounts from the First World War.* Barnsley, S. Yorkshire: Greenhill Books, 2021.

Wakefield, Alan. *Christmas in the Trenches.* Stroud, Gloucestershire: Sutton Publishing Ltd., 2006.

Wedd, A. F. *German Students' War Letters.* London: Methuen & Co., 1929.

Weintraub, Stanley. "The Christmas Truce," *MHQ: The Quarterly Journal of Military History* 5:2 (Winter 1993): 76-85.

_______. *Silent Night: The Story of the World War I Christmas Truce*. New York: The Free Press, 2001.